CW01501232

Beyond The Darkness

*The heartbreak, the healing,
the finding of light*

Dear Abby,

Thank you for all the Support
and for always being an
amazing friend! congratulations
on winning my giveaway ♡

Isobel Askew

BALBOA.PRESS
A DIVISION OF HAY HOUSE

Love,
♡

Balboa Press books may be ordered through booksellers or by contacting:

Balboa Press
A Division of Hay House
1663 Liberty Drive
Bloomington, IN 47403
www.balboapress.co.uk
UK TFN: 0800 0148647 (Toll Free inside the UK)
UK Local: (02) 0369 56325 (+44 20 3695 6325 from outside the UK)

Print information available on the last page.

ISBN: 978-1-9822-8443-5 (sc)
ISBN: 978-1-9822-8444-2 (e)

Balboa Press rev. date: 12/10/2021

Contents

I would like to dedicate this anthology to my younger brother, Alex. Thank you for being the best brother this world has ever known. I would also like to thank my closest friend and biggest supporter, Jess. Finally, a special mention goes to my family and to anyone who has ever believed in me.

"Nothing can dim the light that shines from within."
Maya Angelou

From the time I was a little girl, poetry came as naturally to me as breathing, so writing has remained a constant companion and something I have relied on in tough times. It didn't matter whether people could understand me, or I could understand them, poetry served as a universal language to showcase my raw feelings. Poems exposed my heart, making me vulnerable and honest.

Throughout my entire life people have always told me to look at a glass and see it half full rather than half empty. However, I found that I did not fit into either of those categories. Whilst everyone focused on the contents of the glass, I was too busy fixated on the beauty of how the glass looked. Light bounced off it and made the water sparkle.

Needless to say, I just didn't fit in.

While I was growing up, I was never considered 'popular', perhaps because I was different. The weekends I didn't go out. Instead, I read in the comfort of my own room. For a while, literature was like my best friend. Reading introduced me to a new world that was safer and more beautiful than anything on earth ever could be. It could have been considered a sad revelation, but instead I was determined to create my own magical land. I strongly believe everybody should have a place they can escape when life gets overwhelming or challenging – and here is mine.

My heart and soul in literary form, 'Beyond the Darkness.'

Beyond the darkness, there is a light.

And that light exists within you.

Isobel Askew

Introduction

Good morning, evening, day or night.
I hope you're well and feeling alright.
Welcome to my head. My heart.
An exciting journey about to start.

Year after year around the sun,
Many battles lost and yet to be won.
A simple person and life, you see,
Dreams so big they frighten me.

Please sit down, make yourself at home,
Coffee, Tea? An afternoon scone?
Or would you like sugar? One or two?
No need to hide here, I accept you for you.

You don't understand or maybe you do,
A book sounding old but feeling quite new.
Reminiscent to a lifelong friend,
The perfect day not wanting to end.

Please enjoy and do relax,
Ponder on the world and what it lacks,
Listen to your head and soul,
Let the words make you feel whole.

Infatuation

Infatuation. How do you explain?
The lonely nights, the aching pain,
Midnight pupils dilate so wide,
Makes the adoration impossible to hide.

Your pulse will race,
A touch or embrace.

The scarlet rose of your cheeks
Aching to be plucked.

But is it true?
She was certain she knew.

Was the truth too painful to hear?
For no wrong could be seen of 'darling dear'
Her heart stitched with honest lies.

A vision clouded with the colour red,
Her heart holding on by a single thread,
A concept of three words unsaid,
A day never passed without 'I love you' in her head.

All that mattered, three words, no four.
I don't love you anymore.
Caught in her throat was a breath.
Her heart drowned. Slowly suffocated to death.

Her heart mended itself over time,
The ghost of her ex-lover never left her mind.

But years on, love makes her bloom,
Now love makes her flourish,
Chirping a tune.

Love to her is like a very rainy day,
The storm will always pass,
Love is there to stay.

When You Wish Upon a Star

I dream of the ocean lit up by the moon,
I dream of the songbird chirping its own tune,
I dream of a life beyond what I own,
I dream of my soulmate, not being alone.
I dream of wild passion, worship in the night,
I dream of a miracle, it will be alright,
I dream that the stars will hear my pleas,
I dream of a love as deep as the seas.
I dream of acceptance all over the earth,
I dream of being myself to death from birth,
I dream that no one will stand in my way,
But I guess I'll save dreaming for another day.

The First Time

Playing with my fingers,
Finding it hard to breathe,
Waiting in anticipation,
Asking myself, do I leave?
I've read and I've heard,
But do I know how?
I have never done this before now.
What if I can't make her find bliss?
What if she leaves me without even a kiss?
I've never explored myself this way,
No boys on my mind, not now, not today.
What if I never want to be touched again?
What if my desire is only now, not then?
Is it love? A meaningless fling?
What if it is painful or an uncomfortable thing?
Will I be strong enough to not break apart?
Tell them the truth from the bottom of my heart.
Will it happen or will it simply not?
Preparing myself for nothing, yet a lot.
A bad scenario, a hundred or ten.
Breathe in once... and breathe in again.

Strawberries And Cream

She took my hand, without a doubt,
Never letting me sulk or pout,
She told me I was worth the stars,
She took me dancing, Pubs and Bars,
She touched my hair, caressed it, cared,
My mind became blurry, my vision impaired,
She told me I smelled like a midsummer's dream,
She said I tasted like strawberries and cream.

All For Her

Starlight glitters, the moon shines down,
All for her, always for her.
Flowers bloom and the trees stand tall,
A gift for her, always for her.
The glowing sun lights up her smile,
All for her, always for her.
On the rain kissed green we sit,
Her diamond eyes staring into mine,
The world stops,
Does the sky know its beauty?
No, neither does she.
The world resumes but the stars still shine,
All for her. Always. For her.

Pretty In Pink

'Infantile'
They mutter as I won't have wine to drink.
'Juvenile'
They whisper as I'm head to toe in pink.
As the scrunchies hold my pigtails,
My lips strawberry kissed,
I often stop and wonder,
Will it always be like this?
Restriction becomes an addiction.
Why should I be stopped-?
from wearing bows in my hair.
People stop and stare.
So, I let them.
Is it bravery? Stupidity?
I truly couldn't care.
Or that is what I tell myself,
Every single day,
Fighting back the tears.
All because of my love of
Pink.

Winter Wonderland

Frostbit walks,
Deep, real talks,
The fog of your laugh, I smile.
A mulled wine in hand,
Heating my head,
But you holding my other hand,
Is warming my heart.

My Shooting Star

Knees to my chest,
Fighting off the cold,
Uncontrollable shaking.
Frost? Nerves?
I'm never sure.
All I'm sure of is you.
There you sit
Next to me.
Knees to your chest.
You look cold,
Take my coat, or my hand,
Or if you'd prefer, my heart.
Midnight wakes and all I see is you.
The stars flicker in your eyes,
All I ever see is you.

Unrequited

I told myself I'd stay afloat
This wasn't part of the plan
Falling so deep
I hope I can swim
If I fall too far
I just might give in-
To my heart
Allowing me to be crushed.
The tipping point,
The end,
The last final push.
I love her, I think.
I know. I am sure.
Does she want me?
Need me?
Like me.. or more?
I'm not a good fit,
All the things she is not,
She is perfect, amazing,
Never easily forgot.
A tearing in my chest,
She does not feel the same.
Many nights restless,

Feeling too much pain.
Unrequited and unconventional,
But she still smiles every day,
It would be selfish of me,
To take her smile away.

The Brave Little Snowdrop

(For Mum & Dad)

Awakening in the garden, Amongst crystallised, honeydew
green.
The tiniest baby snowdrop, the prettiest ever to be seen.
To the birdies he was family, to the crawlies he was friend.
Snowy was the happiest and would be until the end.

Drops of winter sprinkled wide and far, swaying in the air,
Kiddie Winkles planting more and treating them with care.
Marshmallows toasting around the fire, Snowy still sees all,
Family trips across the world, Snowy still stands tall.

The sun comes out and melts the ice but Snowy is now wise,
Underneath the summer sun, in a blanket of grass he lies,
Ready for his snooze until the frost returns next year,
Snowy sleeps with a smile on his face feeling no sadness or fear.

The brave little snowdrop, now older but still strong,
He'll say hello at every frost, he'll never be away too long,
The snowdrop holds memories, remaining every day and night.
Keeping all the garden safe and making sure it will all be alright.

A Forbidden Fairy-tale

Once upon a time, I saw stars glisten in your eyes,
I saw the galaxy of your soul,
My heart still flutters when you're nearby,
The final piece made me whole.
My princess charming, perfection and light,
Running from the ball as one, escaping in the night.
My crown long forgotten, the girl I never was,
The most precious thing to me right here.
I look in awe at her beauty, no sunset could compare.
A masterpiece, my goddess, blinding eyes and golden hair.
At the end of the world, we stand hand in hand,
Oh, my love- how I'm lucky to love
The fairest in the land.

The Mistress and The Moon

At dusk, she was a dancer,
The mistress of her craft,
Illuminated by dusty moonlight.
She danced and pranced and jumped,
Leaped, until she could no longer.
At dawn she took her final bow,
Waiting for dusk to return.

Collecting hearts was a hobby,
Not by choice but nonetheless,
Dancing had its downfalls,
Long nights in the shortest dress,
Infatuation polluted her theatre.
Each man leered, a glint in the eye,
She couldn't help but question,
Where, how, when and why?

A burning desire, an intent so dark.

But how she would laugh, scoff and despair,
None of them she wanted or showed any care,
No observer she craved but instead she loathed.

For you see, dear reader, this girl was betrothed.
Betrothed to her true love, sat high in the sky.
They meet again at nightfall, when the clouds say goodbye.

The sun fades away leaving her lit in adoration.
And she would dance.
Oh, how she would dance!

But her posture deceiving,
Her poise was misleading.
She was tired,

Tired of waiting for her love,
Her starlit firefly.
Exhausted of hours spent away from her equal,
her likeness.

She has given up dancing.

No longer she waits and longs for dark,
But you can always find her nearby.
Seated on the frosty sand staring hopefully at the stars,
Her tears frequent,
Her tears, diamonds.

Fallen Angel

Feigning oblivion, they call her naïve,

Although clueless they are of the tricks up her sleeve,

Rosy lips in the morning, at night scarlet red,

As the clock strikes midnight, she'll soon be well fed.

After long nights of screaming,

Feeling glad that she came,

Her throat felt hoarse after screaming her name.

She'll skip into the sun, her pigtails in place,

Holding onto the innocence plastered on her face.

Warrior Tattoos

We didn't need pity,
An apology,
A sign.
All we needed,
Was for you to say
'It will be fine'

Not to show judgement,
Point at our scars,
Someone to kiss them,
Love that they're ours.

Never a sign of weakness,
But bravery and strength.
A long time spent fighting,
Days, weeks, months in length.

The battle leads us here,
Our heads held high,
Now owning our beauty,
Like stars in the sky.

Think

What is beauty?
What do you see?

In the stars in the sky?
When you look at you or me?

What is music?
Or just a sound?

Is it prime happiness?
A penny or a pound?

Do you think it's a story?
Or simply a foolish tale?

Is it just a letter?
Or a useless bit of mail?

Wow, is it a diamond?
Or has the pencil lead gone bad?

Are they quite sane?
Or tell me are they mad?

Eiffel For Her

That girl was curiosity,
She was kind and had my soul,
Hand in hand, side by side,
No longer half but whole.

A happy ending it was not,
I'm afraid her memory of me forgot,
I wish she'd notice me up above,
We'd cross paths and rekindle our love.

This girl was never my lover,
Much more like a friend.
Alas, this was bound to come to an end.
We share memories yet a separate mind,
A bond not bound to never be rebind.

She shares my hair and has my eyes,
But who she is? I do not recognise.
Every day she sits under the Eiffel tower,
She has no interest in fame or power.

Sitting there she reads, absorbing the words,
Surrounded by the sound of culture and birds

The girl I knew once, no longer the same,
I guess that's my fault, I'm partly to blame.

That girl was me yet someone strange,
Someone not afraid that times will change.

A mind that always stayed in place,
And a changing painting upon her face.

Under the Eiffel that is where she will be.
Please know she's her, don't mistake her for me.

The Puppet Master

Dawn to dusk to perpetual night,
Visions clouded by tear drops of light,
Reaching, stretching, straight for the sky,
Collapsing, failing, saying goodbye
To our dreams as they scatter off into the breeze,
Every lifeless vessel down onto their knees.
Head in hands, tears of gold.
Dreams of beauty, getting old,
He fell at dawn, yet no one heard,
Shush! Be quiet! Never say a word!
'You muffled idiot, don't even try'
'Pointless, 'Worthless' lie after lie.
The king was young, old, mad, brave,
'Stand up, be proper'
'No way to behave!'
He digested, consumed, absorbed the debate.
Society's curse, Society's hate.
'Fate' he said as he breathed his last,
Stripped of the present, alive in the past.
Clutching the eternal ruins of time,
Her beauty once a ruby,
Now a dusty nickel or dime.
So close to the ground yet so near the sun,

Yearning for life, no more walking. She'll run.
She stumbles, falls, trips, crashes down.
They laugh and they point,
"My god what a clown!"
A dagger plunged deep into her soul,
Piece by piece the blade takes its toll.
Her years race against her,
The rope starts to tear.
Unsupported all alone,
No one to help up there.
Crumbling, absorbing every vengeful phrase,
I guess it is all a bit blurry now,
A little bit of a daze.
Social pressure screaming so goddamn loud,
Drowning in wars, oppression, prejudice,
A society so very proud.
Landing, aching, hearts are breaking.
Does she finally feel at peace?
Who knew death could be so calm?
Finally, she was free from harm.
As for him he lay cosy asleep,
A beautiful silence,
Not a sound, nor a peep.

I Want to See the Sun

There are scars amongst my stars,
You wrapped them up in silk,
You held them tightly to your skin,
As pale and smooth as milk.
There is a tear on my tapestry,
But still, you sit with care,
Threading a needle, stitching away,
Stroking my touch starved hair.
There is a crack in my heart,
A sharp, mosaic, glint to the eye,
Picking the pieces with delicate ease,
A river of diamond tears, you cry.

There is a gap in my story,
Now pen to paper we write,
A novel so grand, Dickens could not compare,

We made it through the night.

Deep Breaths

Breathe.

Inhale. I swallow my pride.

Breathe.

Exhale. I've nothing to hide.

Breathe.

Inhale. Oh, what have I done?

Breathe.

Exhale. That's it, I'm becoming a nun.

Breathe.

Inhale. Never wear my heart in my mouth.

Breathe.

Exhale. Running north, going south.

Breathe.

Inhale. Then I suddenly see her smile.

Breathe.

Maybe my heart will stay put for a while.

One Cloudy Night

Will I make it too tomorrow?
Pass the night away,
Live my life in colour,
Or a million shades of grey.

Will I make it to the morning?
See the sunshine again,
Listen to the bluebird,
Or will I break before then?

Will I make it to next year?
Five years, fifty too?
Living my days smiling,
Never feeling blue.

C8H11NO2

(For Jess)

You make me laugh,
Dry my tears when I cry,
The heart of an artist,
Never fails to try,
Watering my stems,
So, I grow big and tall,
Funny how before her,
I felt extremely small.
A mind of equations,
Intelligence galore,
My personal solution,
For illness, every cure.
My CO_2, to help me breathe,
She'll always stay and never leave.
My petals wilt when she is far,
But she always shines in every star.
Not connected by blood but by soul,
Who knew I could feel so whole?
My flowers bloom, her potions fizz,
The perfect friendship,
That's what this is.

Goodnight My Friend-
Epilogue

Dusk comes too soon,
The dark reappears,
On your way out I will take your fears,
Just know the world outside the door,
Is big, beautiful and so much more,
Then what we can see every day,
Grab my hand, I'll take you away,
A world of comfort, a magical place,
Life is a saunter, never a race.
Whenever you feel lonely,
Need a friend or two,
Know that these poems will be waiting for you.
But for now, sleep tight,
Put away your phone,
Bask in the moonlight,
No need to wail or groan.
Tuck yourself in tightly,
A metaphorical kiss on the head,
I will be here day and nightly,
Just waiting to be read.

Goodnight my friend.

 Isobel Askew is a writer, poet, LGBTQ+ advocate and climate activist in the United Kingdom. As a lesbian herself, this mental illness warrior is also a strong proponent for racial equality and women's rights. She has been published previously in The Beckindale Poetry Journal, The Cambridge Poetry Journal, From the Heart Poetry Anthology, the 2021 Poets' Yearbook, the October edition of The Crossing Board and gained Elite writer status of the year in The Top 100 Poems of 2021. Aside from writing, Isobel is also a musician, a florist, and a literary fanatic, as well as a lover of Shakespeare's works. In her spare time, one can find Isobel snuggled up with a good book and a pot of tea.

Printed and bound by CPI Group (UK) Ltd, Croydon, CR0 4YY